T0337658

Bert Bielefeld

Office Design

Bert Bielefeld

Office Design

BIRKHÄUSER
BASEL

Contents

Foreword

The design of work space is a demanding task, and rightly so; after all, many people spend a large part of their day in an office. Design parameters include ergonomics, health and safety at work, the right balance between concentrated work and effective communication, through to specific circulation route and space arrangements to suit the respective activity. At the same time as the world of work is changing, there is also a wider range of possible office layout concepts. In addition to traditional office building layouts with individual offices, there are open-plan offices shared by freelancers, and the revolutionary room concepts found mainly in the IT sector, where workplaces are deliberately kept flexible and are defined simply by an electric socket.

In view of this diversity and the exacting requirements pertaining to work space, it is all the more important to provide students with reliable background information. The objective of this book is to facilitate the understanding of the principles of joining together rooms, work areas, and entire office units so that, equipped with this knowledge, they can approach their own office design task in a competent and circumspect way.

General framework conditions and requirements are presented in the fundamentals chapter. The room typologies chapter describes the various types of offices with their secondary functions, and explains how the necessary floor areas can be computed. Finally, the concept and construction of the entire building at a larger scale, and its setting in the architectural context, are considered.

Bert Bielefeld, Editor

Introduction

For many years, the design of office space was dominated by routine considerations with the aim of producing the most efficient use of space while taking into account the requirements of health and safety at work. As a rule, vertical access cores were placed in relation to a standard length of escape route, and the required number of cellular offices or later open-plan office spaces were arranged between the cores.

This process, as described above in very simplified terms, has fundamentally changed. Today, the design of office workplaces has to meet a wide range of requirements. The digitalization and individualization of work increasingly leads to a situation in which office activities can be carried out remotely or, at least, are not tied to a permanent workplace. Many of these activities are paperless and can be performed at any place on laptops or tablets, so that permanently assigned workplaces are no longer always required. In addition, the nature of the work and processes is becoming more and more complex, networked, and specialized, which means that it is becoming ever more important to be able to flexibly switch between team-oriented communication and a focused work environment. At the same time, the boundaries between work and leisure are becoming blurred, which means that here too interactive options have to be created.

This is reflected in the design of office space and buildings, in that flexibly usable and designed spaces are provided for office work. For this reason, the design of office buildings is much more than a schematic arrangement of layouts; rather, it presents a highly tailored task involving building as well as interior design, with the fundamentals having to be established anew for each project. The diversity of organizational concepts and specialized services ensures that this field of work is highly versatile.

Fundamentals

REQUIREMENTS FOR OFFICE WORKPLACES

The requirements for an office workplace can vary a great deal, depending on the respective activity. If the work primarily involves administrative activities with many files and paper documents, the workplaces tend to be static; if the work mostly consists of digital development, it is much easier, depending on the respective requirements, to provide an open choice of workplaces which do not necessarily have to be located in a classic office building. When working with a laptop and an Internet connection, work can be done in an office, a park or café, at home, or in any other environment, provided the surroundings do not interfere with the activity. For this reason, office environments are often designed to accommodate these particular requirements in differently appointed areas.

In terms of the physical aspect of office work, it is rather simple and one-sided but requires a high degree of concentration and mental productivity. And one-sided work, and lack of movement in particular, are often the cause of health problems amongst employees. For this reason office workplaces are a key research subject in work psychology and occupational health and safety, and extensive regulatory instruments have been developed that are intended to protect employees and stimulate optimum performance. These include requirements relating to ergonomics and health and safety in the workplace, as well as the room climate and room acoustics.

Office spaces are becoming more and more diverse, offering high-quality environments in order to foster the well-being and satisfaction of employees. Since office workers spend most of their day at their work space, the working environment should provide for the different phases of the daily routine and for the various tasks — from communication to undisturbed work.

Health and
ergonomics
Another equally important prerequisite is to maintain and promote the health of office workers. The approach to achieving this is based on work/organizational psychology on the one hand and the physical design on the other. The often one-sided work on a computer can lead to health problems over the long term. Excessive eye strain, headaches, tightness and pain in the neck/shoulder area, signs of strain in the lower arms and hands, and an unhealthy posture affecting the spine can result from wrongly designed and inadequately equipped computer workplaces. For this reason, special ergonomic conditions must be provided at computer-

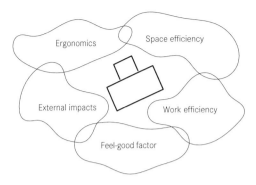

Fig. 1: Requirements of an office workplace

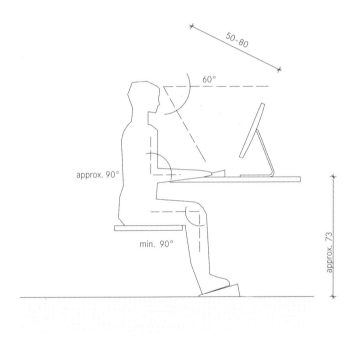

Fig. 2: Ergonomics requirements for a computer workplace

based workplaces. > Fig. 2 Likewise, the room climate, the room acoustics, the lighting, the view to the outside, and many other physical properties play an important role at the workplace. Furthermore, it is important to take measures to avoid sources of injury and risk at the workplace, as well as along the circulation routes and other functional areas.

Satisfaction and well-being   From the point of view of health and safety at work, it is particularly important for a working environment to ensure that office workers are content and feel well at their workplace and in their working environment. To this end, design aspects such as furniture, materials, surfaces, color, and spatial and visual relationships can make a contribution. However, generally speaking, satisfaction is determined by corporate and interpersonal factors such as open and honest communication between different levels of the hierarchy, diverse and responsible duties, and a good sense of collegiality in the team. It follows therefore that although architects can provide a basis, staff satisfaction cannot be achieved through physical measures alone. It is important to develop a sense of the existing non-verbal company culture at an early stage, and to incorporate wishes for the future working environment in the design.

Quietness and communication   The interplay between quiet and concentrated desk work without external stimuli or interference and the communicative exchange between employees and teams must be made possible by physical, functional, and organizational aspects. Within a clearly defined working environment it is possible to create various places for specific communicative needs, such as seating areas with kitchenettes, and meeting rooms, which can be used as needed by staff from defined working areas with allocated workplaces. Likewise, it is also possible to create different work areas and environments that can be used by staff in accordance with their work-related requirements, and which thereby make rigid workplace structures redundant.

This particularly makes sense when the work is more team-based and there is a preponderance of interim phases in which subsequent team meetings have to be worked out on the basis of previously agreed content. It is desirable for working environments that require strong creative potential from employees and a high degree of networking between the different disciplines to be designed to accommodate these activities. By providing meeting rooms, open seating and lounge areas, kitchenettes and coffee bars, and so on, it is possible to create different atmospheres to suit the respective work situations. By contrast, administrative work often requires quieter retreat areas, individual workplaces, or acoustically separable cellular offices. Depending on the specific type of work or service, individual workplaces or team areas are often preferred in this situation.

Comfort and room climate   In order to achieve well-being at the workplace it is necessary to provide adequate comfort; this requires adequate physical conditions such as heat, fresh air, and light in general and, on a personal level, the satisfaction of individual requirements, which can vary a great deal.
> Fig. 3

Tab. 1: Room properties in different types of offices

Room properties			
	Flexibility	Communication	Quietness
Cellular office	–	–	++
Group office	+	++	+
Open-plan office	++	o	–
Combination office	++	++	o

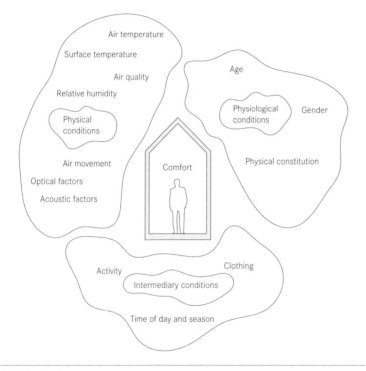

Fig. 3: Comfort in rooms

This may mean that uniformly optimized interior climate conditions are not helpful and can lead to a sense of discomfort, and even health problems, for individual employees. It is much better for office workers to be able to regulate the comfort level at their workplace themselves to meet their own requirements. However, the internal air temperature should never be less than 22 °C, even in winter. Whether cooling or air-conditioning is required during summer periods depends on the individual project.

It is even often the case that mechanical ventilation of rooms is counterproductive, because it may not always be possible to prevent individuals being exposed to drafts. Secondary cooling of rooms (e.g. using cooling ceilings or concrete core activation) often makes sense in new buildings in order to counteract peak values in summer. Owing to the strict energy conservation requirements in new buildings, with the resulting high degree of thermal insulation, and the heat generated by employees and IT devices, particularly in open-plan offices, there is often a greater demand for cooling than for heating, which must be accommo-
■ dated with appropriate technical services.

Ventilation Workplaces in offices must have an adequate supply of fresh air in order to create a comfortable working atmosphere and to keep the concentration of noxious substances and odors in the air low. > Tab. 2 Offices can be ventilated via natural window ventilation or via a mechanical ventilation system. In cellular offices, individually controlled window ventilation is often the preferred option, provided this is possible within the energy conservation concept and noise pollution from outside (e.g. busy roads) is relatively low. In rooms with larger numbers of employees, window ventilation can be problematic because it may not be possible to accommodate conflicting individual requirements, and a mechanical ventilation system is therefore recommended.

Tab. 2: Examples of air exchange rates in different rooms

Room type	Air exchange in h^{-1}
Offices	2.0–6.0
Meeting rooms	6.0–12.0
Assembly rooms	5.0–10.0
Sanitary areas	3.0–6.0
Canteens	6.0–8.0

■ Tip: The parameters for room climate, comfort, and air quality are dealt with in *Basics Room Conditioning* by Oliver Klein and Jörg Schlenger. The volume also discusses different concepts for cooling, heating, and air-conditioning buildings.

When carrying out focused work in particular, a quiet working atmos- phere is important. This can be negatively influenced by external factors, such as noise from the outside, or by internal factors arising from neighboring workplaces. For this reason, individual workplaces with a requirement for quiet must be adequately protected using acoustically effective measures or acoustic separating elements. In offices with a lot of conversation, customer presence, or telephone calls, such as call centers in particular, the design of room acoustics is a basic requirement for the proper function of the space. As a rule, the primary approach is to reduce excessive numbers of acoustic sources of noise, to ensure that speech can be understood, and to limit reverberation times. To meet the above requirements, the surfaces of floors, walls, and ceilings are lined with acoustically effective material, which may also be supplemented by additional absorber elements in the form of ceiling sails, mobile partitions, or office furniture.

Lighting is another important design parameter, usually met by in- cluding a balanced combination of natural and artificial light sources. > Fig. 4 and Tab. 3 Windows can provide adequate daylight to workplaces close to the facade; however, the depth of daylight penetration is usually limited to 5–7 m, even in the case of floor-to-ceiling windows, which means

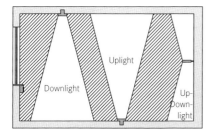
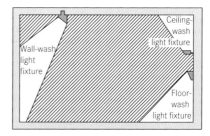
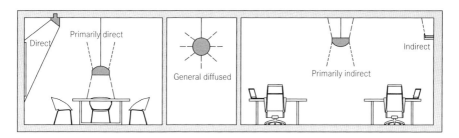

Fig. 4: Directed and undirected sources of light in a room

that workplaces farther away from the facade require permanent artificial lighting. A rule of thumb states that with an open proportion of 60% (i.e. windows above sill level), natural light can be provided up to a depth of 1.5 times the height of the window.

For computer workplaces it is particularly important to provide individual glare protection, in addition to any external solar screening controlled elsewhere, in order to create an environment that is consistently free from glare. Artificial lighting should ideally include general glare-free
■ background lighting and an individually controllable workplace light.

Tab. 3: Guide values for the light intensity in various kinds of rooms (to DIN 12464-1)

Type of room	E_m in lx
Circulation areas and corridors	100
Staircases, escalators	150
Canteens, kitchenettes	200
Staff rooms	100
Sanitary rooms	500
Conference and meeting rooms	500
Archives	200
Offices (writing, reading, data processing)	500

■ Tip: The different requirements for daylight and artificial light are dealt with in detail in *Basics Lighting Design* by Roman Skowranek. The book also explains various concepts for controlling and directing light for rooms with greater depth.

DESIGN OF OFFICE WORKPLACES

The basic components of an office workplace are a desk and a chair Elements of an office workplace which, where required, may be supplemented by storage and shelving, and IT and telecommunications equipment, as well as visitor/meeting areas. The range extends from highly space-optimized workplaces, e.g. in call centers (> Fig. 5), which consist of nothing more than a work cubicle with screen, keyboard, and telephone connection, through to generous individual offices with shelves and a seating area with table for meetings. > Fig. 6

Fig. 5: Furniture in a call center

Fig. 6: Example of an exclusive individual office

Depending on the requirements, elements can be arranged freely in the room in order to create an agreeable working environment. However, in a space-optimized approach, minimum sizes and distances must be observed. The standard size of a desk is 160 × 80 cm or 180 × 90 cm. Space for movement of at least 100 cm must be provided in front of the desk. The standard depth of shelves and sideboards is 40 cm, although enclosed cupboards can be up to 60 cm deep.

On this basis, the space requirement per workplace can be calculated. While extremely frugal cubicles may need significantly less than $2\,m^2$ per employee, high-quality and luxurious offices can be designed with 20–$30\,m^2$ per workplace. > Fig. 7 and Tab. 4

In addition to the space requirement for the desk and chair, additional space must be allowed for cupboards, document and meeting tables, movement areas, and circulation routes within the office rooms. > Tab. 5 and Fig. 8

For office buildings with identical workplaces, once a sample workplace has been designed, including all secondary spaces, one can calculate the overall floor area required by multiplying the number of employees by the number of identical workplaces.

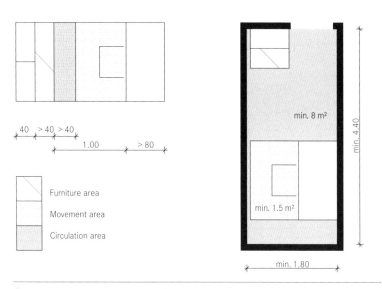

40   > 40 > 40
1.00   > 80

Furniture area

Movement area

Circulation area

min. 8 m²

min. 1.5 m²

min. 4.40

min. 1.80

Fig. 7: Minimum space requirements for an individual workplace

Tab. 4: Rough minimum values for room sizes

Space requirement for one person	≥ 8 m²
Space requirement for two persons	≥ 13 m²
Space requirement for three persons	≥ 18 m²
Each additional workplace	+ ≥ 5 m²

Tab. 5: Areas required for and around desks (as per ArbStättV [Workplaces Ordinance])

Unobstructed movement area at the desk	1.50 m²
Minimum depth of personally assigned workplace	1.00 m
Minimum depth of other workplaces	0.80 m
Minimum depth for visitor/meeting tables/desks	0.80 m

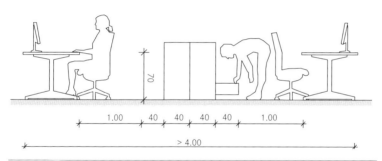

Fig. 8: Minimum distances at workplaces

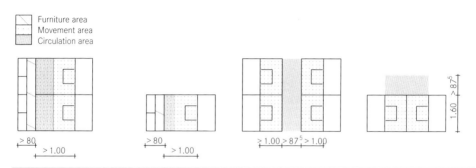

Furniture area
Movement area
Circulation area

Fig. 9: Dimensions of workspace modules for single and double workplaces

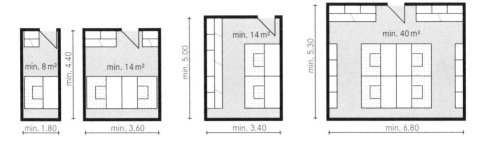

Fig. 10: Minimum floor areas of office rooms

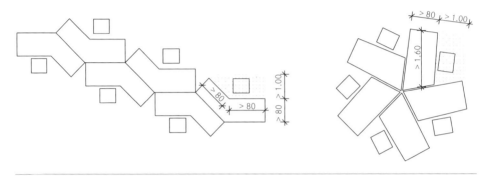

Fig. 11: Space-saving desk concepts

Room typologies

OFFICE TYPES

Depending on the number of workplaces, a distinction is made between the different types of office rooms. These are:

— Individual/cellular offices: approx. 1–4 persons
— Group offices: approx. 5–25 persons
— Open-plan offices: over 25 persons
— Combi-offices: variable depending on requirements
— Non-territorial work environments: variable depending on requirements

Individual or cellular offices are separate, distinct office rooms arranged in sequence along circulation corridors. They can accommodate up to a maximum of 4 workplaces. Depending on the spacing of the fit-out grid and the number of workplaces, they are between 2.60 m and 5.00 m wide, and between 5.00 m and 6.00 m deep. One- and two-person offices have a high space requirement per user. In practice, cellular offices are often combined with other room types. As a rule, the workplaces in cellular offices are assigned to permanent employees for the longer term, but they can also be intended as retreat rooms for concentrated working, or for external consultants or auditors. In order to improve the communication and connecting routes between individual workplaces, it is possible to provide intermediate doors to cellular offices; however, this requires additional circulation space within the rooms. In office buildings where there are only cellular offices, meeting rooms and communication areas, such as staff kitchens, become rather more important for the purpose of maintaining good communication. > Fig. 12

Individual/
cellular offices

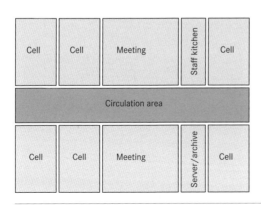

Fig. 12: Diagram of a cellular office arrangement

The term "group office" is used for offices with about 5 to 25 employees; they are distinct units arranged along circulation corridors, either open to these or separated by partition walls. Depending on the spacing of the building fit-out grid and the number of workplaces, they are between 7.00 m and 30.00 m wide, and between 5.00 m and 10.00 m deep. A group office is an intermediate form of office between a cellular and open-plan office, and represents an attempt to combine the advantages of these two types of rooms. Compact furniture and half-height separation walls make efficient use of the space and can create visual and acoustic separation between groups of desks that are not far from the comfort of an individual workplace. Activities that would have an

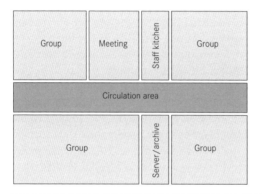

Fig. 13: Diagram of a group office arrangement

Fig. 14: Example of group office furnishings with workbays

impact on the concentration of colleagues can be located in additional rooms, such as meeting and conference rooms or small cellular offices, where staff can conduct meetings or make longer phone calls. > Fig. 13 Another option for dealing with the problem of acoustic interference is to install specially designed work cubicles with sound-absorbing separating walls. Group offices enhance communication and make it possible to allocate tasks in an uncomplicated manner. There is no need to leave the room for smaller meetings or for making arrangements with colleagues.

Where services are installed in floor boxes, the desk layout should be designed at an early stage because floor boxes should not be located in the area of the office where chair castors will move around or in the legroom beneath the desk.

Combi-offices combine cellular or group offices located along a window facade with an additional combi-zone in the interior of the building. As a rule, the additional combi-zone is between 5.00 m and 7.00 m deep, and also serves as access to the offices along the periphery. It can be used to accommodate permanent functions such as sanitary units and stairwells, or for other variable functions depending on requirements. By providing communication and meeting zones, media and storage areas, etc., it is possible to design combi-offices very flexibly and to suit specific

Combi-offices

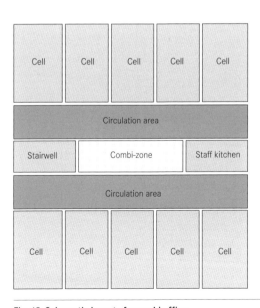

Fig. 15: Schematic layout of a combi-office

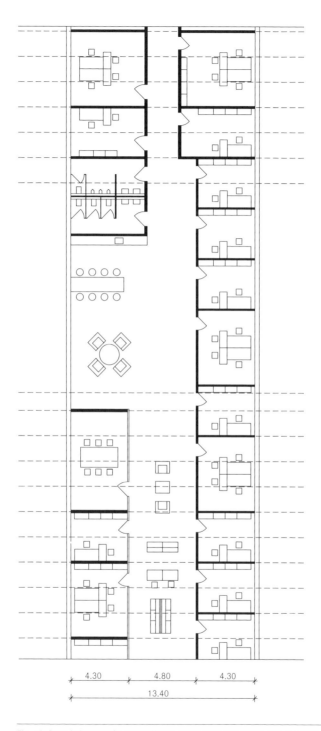

4.30　　　　　4.80　　　　4.30

13.40

Fig. 16: Sample layout of combi-office with an area extending into an office landscape

Downlight

Fig. 17: Example of furniture layout in a combi-zone

needs related to the work processes. In order to ensure that daylight reaches the combi-zones, it is important to provide transparent corridor separating walls. The space efficiency of combi-offices largely depends on whether additional communication and staff areas with a large space requirement are created in the combi-zone, or whether it is primarily occupied by ancillary functions which would otherwise have to be provided along an external wall. As a rule, the latter results in more compact and hence more efficient building forms.

Open-plan offices are often work landscapes designed without a corridor which may well be over 1000 m^2 in size. Depending on how close together the workplaces are arranged, they can be highly efficient in terms of use of the square area, but require very extensive data/electrical installations, as well as ventilation/air-conditioning, which means that — in most cases — greater room heights need to be provided to accommodate suspended ceilings or raised floors. The biggest design challenge in such rooms is the air-conditioning and the handling of the acoustic problems in order to ensure adequate employee satisfaction. Open-plan offices can range in depth, although experience has shown that no workplace should be more than 20 m away from an external window. It is also important to remember that, in spite of the corridor-less layout, it is normally a statutory requirement to provide escape and rescue routes within the open-plan office.

Open-plan offices

In most cases, individual work and functional areas are created by using mobile separating walls and furniture systems in open-plan offices in order to be able to make flexible use of the space in accordance with the current requirements. Furthermore, important design elements for quiet working or telephone conversations are retreat and communication zones which, as a rule, increase the comfort level and hence employee acceptance. > Fig. 18

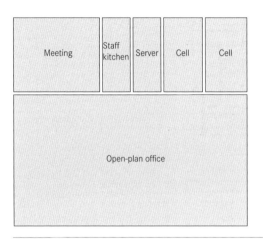

Fig. 18: Schematic layout of an open-plan office

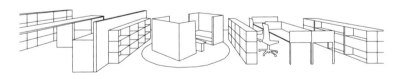

Fig. 19: Example of an open-plan office furniture layout

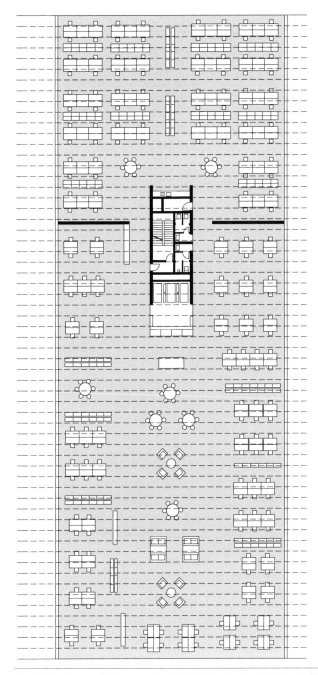

Fig. 20: Sample layout of an open-plan office (open-plan furnishing and office landscape)

As part of the development towards more and more individual and flexible ways of working, including the full digitalization of work processes, new concepts are created again and again, which can be summarized under the term "non-territorial work environments." This includes an approach in which workplaces are no longer permanently assigned to certain employees, but are used flexibly as demand arises (examples are a flexible office, desk sharing). In addition, there are concepts that focus on completely new ways of working (e.g. teleworking, digitalization, company-internal think tanks), making classic workplace situations largely redundant.

The starting point is usually the different work situations: from concentrated work phases with as little disturbance as possible through to open communication and team phases, during which concepts are developed, results are discussed, and mid-career training takes place. Other important aspects may be customer involvement or the presentation of the work and development process to the outside in order to present innovative company structures or to attract qualified personnel. Non-territorial work environments therefore require a wide range of work and communication zones, which means that classic forms of offices are often completely dissolved. > Fig. 21 Many custom-designed concepts exist that try to provide relaxed and creative working conditions, sometimes involving settings related to lifestyle and leisure. The idea is to blur the boundaries between work and leisure. All the office types discussed above can be integrated into these concepts without any problems, although as a rule non-territorial concepts are based on open-plan structures.

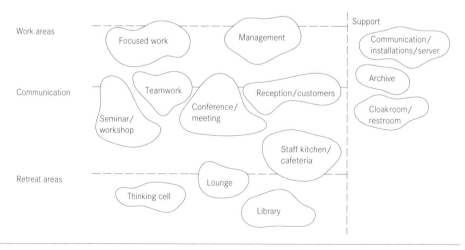

Fig. 21: Schematic layout of functions of a non-territorial work environment

Combi-zones and the interior areas of open-plan offices and non-territorial work environments, with their low levels of natural light, are often used to accommodate various secondary support functions rather than permanent workplaces. There are many possible options:

— Open communication and lounge areas
— Meeting rooms
— Staff kitchens with staff seating areas
— Media areas for fax, printer, copier, server, and other IT equipment
— Cloakrooms
— Archive and storage areas, libraries
— Telephone areas, thinking cells, other temporary workplaces
— Sanitary cores
— Circulation areas with staircases and elevators
— Service installation ducts

Some of these, such as those requiring services installations, are normally fixed, but others can be arranged more flexibly with the help of built-in furniture and other custom-made elements > Chapter Room typologies, Meetings and communication in order to provide zoning in large spaces and to increase the flexibility of use and communication options.

Where workplaces with customer contact have to be designed, the requirements described in the chapter on Fundamentals must be accommodated with the needs of customer interaction. This is especially true in buildings with a high customer traffic, such as banks, customer centers, or public services, where workplaces are often located in large rooms or halls, along with waiting areas and information facilities. In such cases, it is necessary to not only provide adequate environmental conditions, but also ensure a certain amount of privacy and safety for the employees. In addition, the public areas must be equipped with information counters, waiting areas, drink dispensers, sanitary facilities, and so on. There should also be separate provision of barrier-free (accessible) sanitary facilities and guidance (directions, mapping) systems for employees and visitors/customers.

MEETINGS AND COMMUNICATION

Meeting and communication areas are important elements in every office in order to ensure smooth work processes. They can either be integrated openly in the respective office units, added in the form of decentralized meeting rooms or areas, or provided centrally in dedicated organizational units as seminar and meeting units.

The variety of integrated communication and meeting areas ranges from small meeting tables with two chairs in cellular offices through to differently designed, non-territorial communication spaces in open-plan offices. Communication areas integrated into open-plan arrangements may include solutions from small meeting cubicles as pieces of furniture > Fig. 22 through to environments reflecting certain subjects or leisure themes. > Fig. 23 The details of the design largely depend on the respective uses and may be suited for discussions, negotiations, business meetings, and/or giving presentations.

Meeting rooms are usually designed for just that single function, and offer a quiet and sometimes also distinct space for meetings between employees or with customers. They may be located centrally or be assigned to departments, floors, or individual persons, which also determines their location in the building. Where visitors are expected frequently, it is advisable to locate these rooms where access to them is direct and straightforward so that visitors do not have to be guided through internal departments. In view of the various requirements of different groups and the considerable space requirement of meeting rooms, it often makes sense to provide flexible ways of dividing the room so that smaller meetings can take place regularly but large gatherings can also be accommodated. The size of the meeting room ultimately depends on the maximum number of participants and the furnishing. > Fig. 24

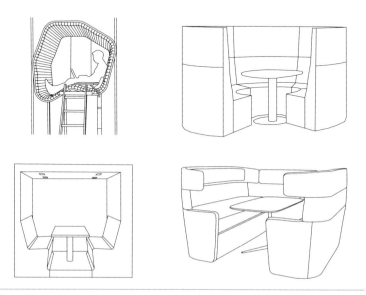

Fig. 22: Examples of seating furniture for use in combi-zones

Fig. 23: Examples of design for larger integrated communication areas

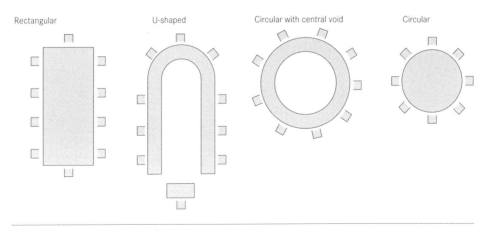

Rectangular U-shaped Circular with central void Circular

Fig. 24: Furnishing options for meeting rooms

31

Meeting rooms should always include technical infrastructure. From a size of approx. 4 to 6 seats, it is obligatory to provide projectors, screens, black-out facilities, and network connections. It also makes sense to provide a kitchenette or self-service coffee bar close to the meeting room.

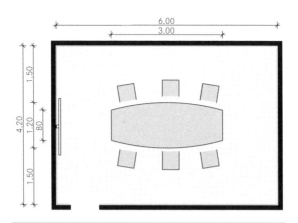

Fig. 25: Furnishing example for a small meeting room

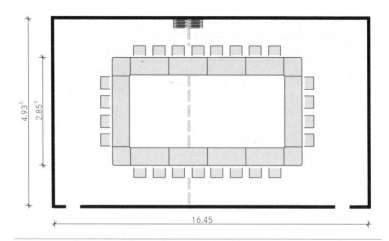

Fig. 26: Furnishing example for a small conference room

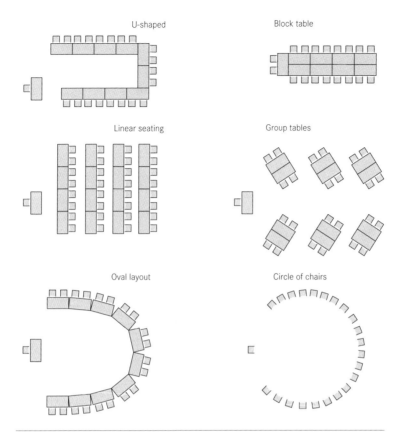

U-shaped

Block table

Linear seating

Group tables

Oval layout

Circle of chairs

Fig. 27: Furnishing options for conference rooms

If several meeting rooms are provided at a central location in the building, it is possible to provide independent seminar and conference areas that may also have the benefit of separate access and services installations. When the intention is to organize larger events, it is a prerequisite that the meeting and conference rooms can be combined to form a larger space. Arranging the access to a meeting and conference area via the main foyer helps to organize and manage training events or events with customer contacts. Seminar and conference areas should have their own separate sanitary units, including accessible restroom, break areas, and coffee and snack bar, as well as storage rooms for any movable seating and equipment.

Seminar and conference areas

CIRCULATION AND SERVICES

As a rule, office buildings are accessed via a main entrance, vertical circulation cores, and corridors. When the use of the building is of a mono-functional nature, open areas are possible, which may also flow into each other. Where several units are accessed via one entrance, access should be arranged in two stages, via a central public entrance and then one that only serves the unit. Where an office building also has a representational function and has to accommodate visitor traffic, access is often arranged via a multi-story foyer with reception area and further access to all visitor and meeting areas.

Barrier-free accessibility

Regardless of the type and use of an office building, access to and use of all areas should be barrier-free. This means that all areas are accessible to wheelchair users without having to use staircases, if necessary via elevators, that all circulation routes and doors are wide enough, and that it is possible, at any time, to set up wheelchair user workplaces with adequate space around them. > Figs. 28 and 29 For visually impaired people it is necessary to provide good orientation in the building and a high-contrast and low-glare interior. In addition to providing specific rooms, such as disabled restrooms, it is very important for the designer to make it possible for disabled persons to reach all rooms without encountering obstacles.

○

Entrance areas

Entrance areas can be designed as simple lobbies with access control or as prestigious spaces with a number of secondary functions. > Fig. 30 They determine the first impression when entering the building, and are therefore an important part of the company's corporate identity. As a rough guide, a space requirement of 0.2 to 0.6 m^2 per employee workplace can be assumed.

Entrance areas often contain a workplace, which is also subject to all regulations pertaining to health and safety at work. It is common to protect access points with security systems/access control systems, which define the boundary between publicly accessible areas and the internal staff area. Where waiting areas are provided in the foyer, there should also be sanitary facilities. In some cases, reception areas have

○ **Note**: Further requirements for barrier-free design can be found in the following chapters, as well as in detail in *Basics Barrier-free Planning* by Isabella Skiba and Rahel Züger. The book explains the requirements for specific rooms for use by people with different disabilities.

direct access to a mailroom and parcel storage area. Buildings with high customer/visitor traffic require direction and mapping systems, and a clear circulation layout is very important in order to facilitate orientation. Where parking spaces are provided on a lower floor, there should be a straightforward route to the entrance area that takes into account the security concept of the building. In some cases it may be necessary to provide separate elevators just connecting underground parking areas with the foyer.

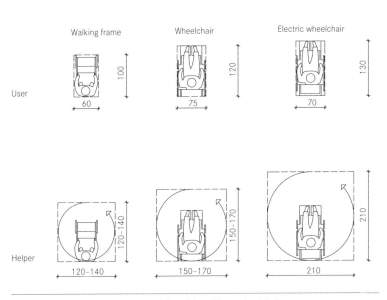

Fig. 28: Movement areas of people with walking aids or wheelchairs

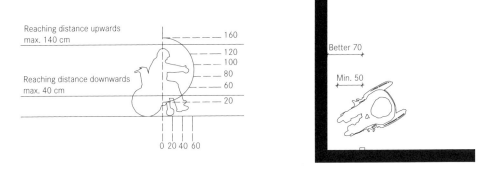

Fig. 29: Reaching distances for wheelchair users

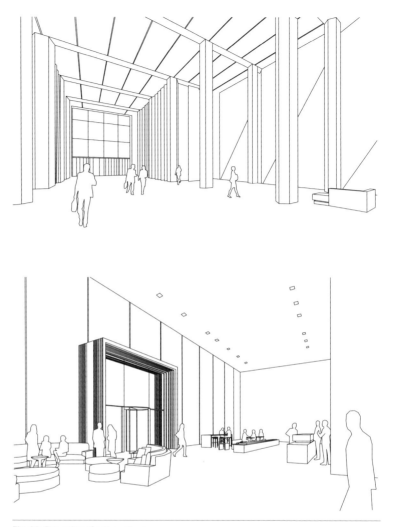

Fig. 30: Examples of entrance areas

Access to the vertical circulation system should be easy to find and should be directly accessible from the entrance zone with lobby and reception or porter. The number of elevators required is determined by the applicable building code; however, it may be necessary to provide additional or larger elevators where significant numbers of visitors are expected or to reduce waiting times. > Fig. 31 If the design provides open access from the foyer, the requirements for escape and rescue routes must be taken into account, which can mean that additional stairwells have to be provided.

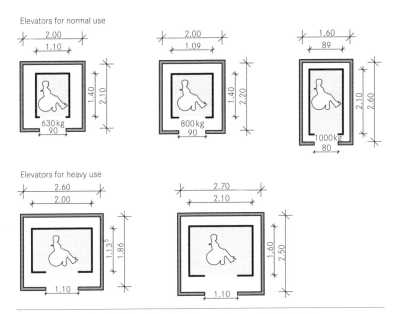

Elevators for normal use

Elevators for heavy use

Fig. 31: Guidelines for the size of elevators in accordance with DIN 15309

Tab. 6: Minimum width of circulation routes as per ASR A1.8

Clear minimum width of circulation routes for the number of persons served	
up to 5 persons	0.875 m
up to 20 persons	1.00 m
up to 200 persons	1.20 m
up to 300 persons	1.80 m
up to 400 persons	2.40 m

The function of corridors is to provide access, to serve as necessary escape and rescue routes or, depending on the type of office, they can also be used as staff areas and communication zones. With integrated concepts such as combi-zones and open-plan offices, it is important to make sure that the minimum clear width of these is maintained > Tab. 6 and that the fire loads, which cannot be avoided, comply with the fire protection concept. The same applies to doors between fire compartments — the minimum clear width must be complied with. When designing the width of corridors and escape routes, it is imperative to take into account the opening direction of doors, as this can have an impact on the width of corridors and is an important consideration for barrier-free access. > Figs. 32 and 33

Corridors in office areas

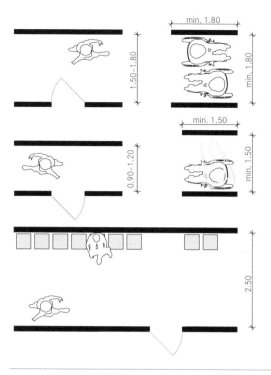

Fig. 32: Minimum width of corridors used for different functions

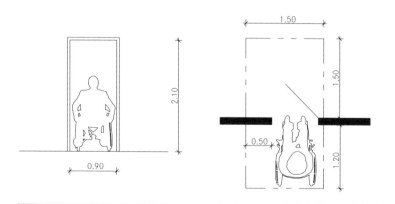

Fig. 33: Minimum dimensions of doors and movement areas for barrier-free access

Tab. 7: Maximum rescue route lengths at workplaces as per ASR A2.3

Room type	Maximum length
In normal workrooms	35.00 m
For rooms with a fire risk, with automatic fire extinguishing devices	35.00 m
For rooms with a fire risk, without automatic fire extinguishing devices	25.00 m

The distances between access cores and fire compartments are determined based on the regulations for the maximum length of escape and
rescue routes, which are usually defined by the local building regulations.
These distances in turn affect the typology of the building layout.

Fire compartments

Fire compartments are formed by room-enclosing walls, ceilings, and
doors that ensure a certain resistance to fire and smoke in order to limit
any fire to the respective fire compartment during the evacuation of the
building. In Germany, the maximum permitted distance between escape
route stairwells is 35 m. > Tab. 7 In most cases, escape from the building must
be possible via two independent routes just in case one route is obstructed
by fire. The maximum size of fire compartments is 40 m × 40 m, and man-
datory corridors have to be separated into sections with a maximum length
of 30 m by self-closing smoke control (fire) doors. This leads to a number
of options in the layout design and arrangement of building compartments.

ANCILLARY ROOMS

In addition to circulation areas and actual work spaces, office buildings need various ancillary rooms and functions. These are the usual
ones:

— Staff kitchens and dining areas; canteens if appropriate
— Staff rooms if appropriate
— Sanitary facilities
— First-aid room
— Stores and archives
— Logistics and utility rooms such as server rooms and janitorial rooms

Every office unit/floor should have the benefit of a staff kitchen that
is easy for all employees to reach. These are often arranged close to the
sanitary cores on all floors, usually above each other in order to simplify
the installation of pipes. The minimum standard for a staff kitchen includes a small row of kitchen furniture with cabinets, refrigerator, dish-
washer, coffee machine, kettle, microwave, and so on. However, many
companies integrate staff kitchens in larger communication areas in the
form of a self-serve coffee bar. > Figs. 34 and 35

Staff kitchens

Fig. 34: Example of a staff kitchen in a combi-zone

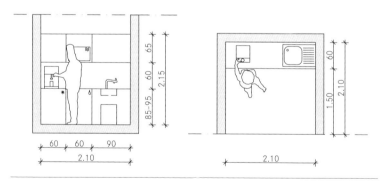

Fig. 35: Minimum dimensions of a staff kitchen as a separate room

Tab. 8: Minimum dimensions of a staff kitchen as a separate room

Minimum distances to be provided in kitchens	
Distance between two rows of kitchen furniture opposite each other (worktops)	1.20 m
Distance between row of kitchen furniture and the opposite wall	1.20 m
Distance between two rows of kitchen furniture opposite each other, for wheelchair users	1.50 m
Distance between row of kitchen furniture and the opposite wall, for wheelchair users	1.50 m
Distance between row of kitchen furniture and adjoining wall	3 cm
Distance between row of kitchen furniture and door/window reveal	10 cm

If staff rooms are required, a practical solution is to combine a staff Staff rooms room with a staff kitchen in order to give employees the opportunity to eat a meal during their break. There should be sufficient seating and also a view to the outside. > Fig. 36 Separate staff rooms are required in situations where the workplaces are located directly in the customer area and it is not possible for employees to take their breaks without interference.

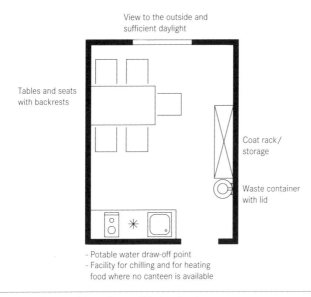

View to the outside and sufficient daylight

Tables and seats with backrests

Coat rack/ storage

Waste container with lid

- Potable water draw-off point
- Facility for chilling and for heating food where no canteen is available

Fig. 36: Staff room with small row of kitchen furniture

In larger office buildings and where there are no restaurants close to the building, it is possible to include an in-house canteen or cafeteria in the design to ensure adequate provisions for employees, or to improve employee satisfaction by offering high-quality facilities. In terms of organization, canteens are independent units which, in addition to the dining area, require an extensive and complex kitchen area. > Fig. 37 A rough guide for the floor space required for a canteen is approx. $1.00-1.5\,m^2$ of dining room space and approx. $1.2-1.6\,m^2$ of kitchen area per seat.

It is usual to group sanitary rooms in office buildings together, either by floor or by section; sanitary cores are conveniently located close to vertical pipe installations (in most cases close to the vertical circulation core). The established layout of sanitary cores includes separate facilities for women and men, with a wheelchair-accessible restroom in between; in many cases, a janitorial room will also be included in the core. > Fig. 38 The number of toilets and washbasins required is specified in the Workplace Ordinance. > Tab. 9 Some employers also provide shower facilities for their employees (e.g. for sports activities during the lunch break).

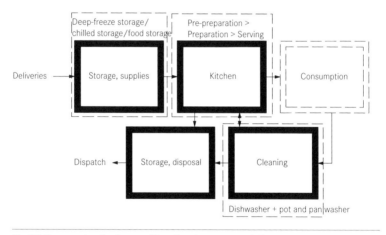

Fig. 37: Diagram showing layout of functions in a commercial kitchen

O **Note**: It is not possible here to discuss in detail the requirements of commercial kitchens. The design of commercial kitchens and canteens is dealt with in detail in the book *Planning Architecture*, published by Birkhäuser.

In addition to the sanitary facilities for employees, additional guest restrooms must be provided in appropriate locations, such as in the foyer, close to meeting areas, or in waiting zones.

As a rule, but depending on local regulations, a separate first-aid room of approx. 20 m^2 is required from 1000 employees upwards; this is used to provide first-aid in a medical emergency prior to the arrival of the ambulance. If possible, this room should be located on the ground floor close to the entrance area.

First-aid room

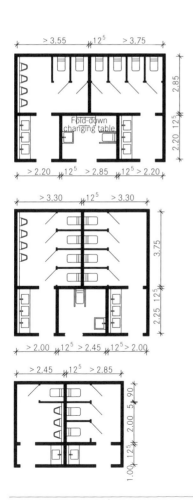

Fig. 38: Space requirements for sanitary facilities

Tab. 9: Number of toilets, urinals, and hand lavatories required in accordance with ASR A4.1

Number of male employees	Number of toilets	Number of urinals	Hand lavatories	Number of female employees	Number of toilets	Hand lavatories
up to 5	1	1	1	up to 5	1	1
up to 10	1	1	1	up to 10	1	1
up to 25	2	2	1	up to 25	2	2
up to 50	3	3	1	up to 50	3	2
up to 75	5	5	2	up to 75	4	3
up to 100	6	6	2	up to 100	5	3
up to 130	7	7	3	up to 130	6	4
up to 160	8	8	3	up to 160	7	4
up to 190	9	9	3	up to 190	8	5
up to 220	10	10	4	up to 220	9	6
up to 250	11	11	4	up to 250	10	7

Storage and archive rooms

The difference between storage rooms and an archive is that the former is used to store regularly used material, while the latter is used for storing files that are rarely used. Both types of rooms can be located in a central place or decentralized, i.e. spread throughout the building. For example, files may be stored within a department in combi-zones, or in a central archive in the basement. The size of storage rooms depends largely on the required function. On the upper floors of buildings, rooms with poor daylighting (e.g. next to circulation cores) can also be used for storage, especially for consumables. Chair and/or furniture storage facilities must be located near conference and meeting areas.

IT Server room

Depending on the IT network architecture, server rooms may be located either externally or within the building, usually in a protected location in the basement. Where cable-based data technology has been provided, vertical distribution ducts are needed, as well as distribution rooms for the data network on each floor. In smaller systems, it is also common to arrange server cabinets inside other rooms; in that case, it is important to take into account the considerable noise and heat generated by the server.

Plant/utility rooms

In larger buildings, plant/utility rooms for ventilation, heating, utility connections, and so on are often grouped together, either in stories below ground or in attic floors. For cost reasons, ventilation plants are often located on the roof, exposed to the weather.

Janitorial rooms

A janitorial room must be provided on each floor and in each separately leased unit; this should have a slop sink and water draw-off point.

Design concept and building types

Although it is possible to develop initial layout designs on the basis of the room typologies and functional areas described above, a fully functional design has to take into account numerous additional parameters. These include the urban framework conditions, the context of the plot (land), the functional relationships, the building volume, the circulation system, and the structural system of the building. These parameters are explained below to help designers integrate these complex factors in the design of office buildings. ∎

DETERMINING AREA AND VOLUME

The room schedule and requirement profiles for the design of the office and ancillary spaces are developed based on the functional requirements. However, at the start of the design process, it is necessary to carry out a rough check as to what volume/floor area can be accommodated on the available building land, and what volume is required to accommodate the specified number of workplaces.

As a starting point, the number of employees to be accommodated must be multiplied by the space requirement per employee. Even though

Office space – ancillary areas

Tab. 10: Design data for different organizational forms of offices

Room type	Persons	Room depth	Clear room height
Cellular office	1 to 4	5 to 6 m	≥ 2.50 m
Group office	5 to 25	5 to 10 m	≥ 2.50 m to ≥ 3.00 m
Small groups	5 to 8	5 to 7.5 m	≥ 2.50 m to ≥ 2.75 m
Large groups	8 to 25	7.5 to 10 m	≥ 2.75 m to ≥ 3.00 m
Combi-office (cellular and group offices)	1 to 25	4 to 10 m	≥ 2.75 m to ≥ 3.00 m
Combi-office (combi-zone, circulation area)		5 to 7 m	
Open-plan office	25 to > 100	15 to 40 m	≥ 3.00 m to ≥ 3.25 m

∎ **Tip:** The volume *Basics Design Ideas* by Bert Bielefeld and Sebastian El khouli presents students with various options for developing a design solution. In addition to general suggestions about creative processes and how to develop a design approach, various sources of inspiration for a design idea are suggested.

a minimum floor area per employee of 8 m^2 has been mentioned, significantly more space per employee should be allowed in higher quality offices. For cellular offices, it is common to provide between 13 and 18 m^2, while in more efficient office layouts, such as in group and open-plan offices, the floor area per employee is smaller.

Once the average space requirement per employee has been determined, calculating the overall space requirement for just the workplaces is a matter of simple multiplication. In addition, the space requirement for ancillary functions, circulation areas, and construction space has to be computed. Where extensive ancillary functions are provided, such as centralized meeting and conference units, the space requirement for these should be determined separately. For ancillary areas close to the workplaces, such as staff kitchens, restrooms, storerooms, smaller communication zones and stairwells, it is possible to either make a general addition to the space requirement or to calculate the specific size of the ancillary areas using schematic layout drawings. > Fig. 39 Provided an idea about the general layout is already in place, using drawings is significantly more precise.

An additional floor area of 15 to 30% can be included for construction and installation areas such as walls, pillars, facades and ducts in order to obtain the gross floor area on the basis of the usable floor area. The gross floor area is then divided by the number of stories to establish the footprint area of the building, and this is then positioned on the available building land.

Height from floor to floor, height of rooms

In order to calculate the volume of the building and its resulting height, the calculation of floor space described above must be multiplied by a dimension for height. The height of rooms and from floor to floor

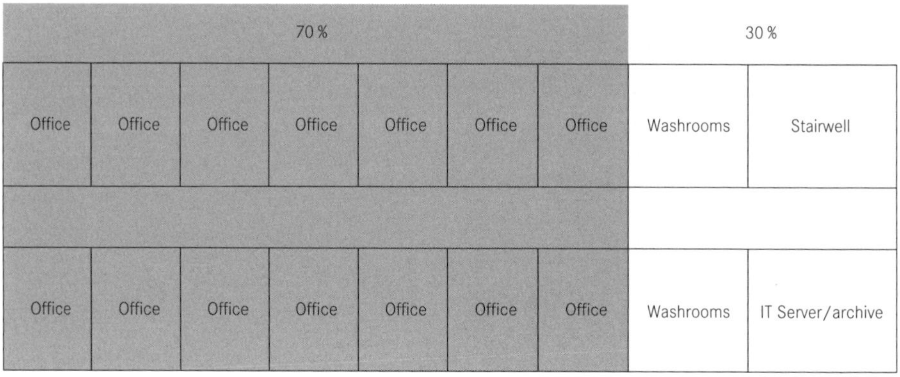

70 %							30 %	
Office	Office	Office	Office	Office	Office	Office	Washrooms	Stairwell
Office	Office	Office	Office	Office	Office	Office	Washrooms	IT Server / archive

Fig. 39: Schematic computation of space requirements for ancillary areas

Tab. 11: Minimum clear room heights for office workplaces as per ASR A1.2

Floor area up to 50 m²	≥ 2.50 m
Floor area up to 100 m²	≥ 2.75 m
Floor area up to 2000 m²	≥ 3.00 m
Floor area over 2000 m²	≥ 3.25 m
Clear room height for workplaces and circulation areas where there are sloping ceilings	≥ 2.50 m

must comply with minimum legal requirements, and should also take into account principles of proportion. Depending on the size of the room, a clear minimum height of 2.50–3.25 m should be provided. > Tab. 11 However, if this is applied to an open-plan office, the visual effect is of a rather squat room with poor amenity quality. The story height of each floor is determined by the room with the greatest room height; therefore, this room needs to be established in the first step.

To calculate the story height based on the room height, the structural elements (floor slabs, downstands), as well as other elements of the construction and of the installation, such as screed, suspended ceiling and void for services installations, must be taken into account. Depending on the specific design, the construction height (finished ceiling + floating screed) adds up to at least 40 cm, while the overall height, including voids and installation elements (suspended ceiling incl. ventilation installation, concrete floor, raised floor incl. space for ventilation and data network installation), can add up to more than 100 cm. > Fig. 40

These calculation examples, although initially very approximate, are useful in giving an initial sense of the volume to be accommodated on the building plot, and in providing an initial idea for the design of the building.

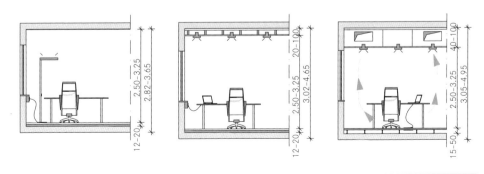

Fig. 40: Determining the story height, including different installation arrangements

FUNCTIONAL CONTEXT

Analysis of
internal processes

Once the total required floor area and the room schedule have been established, it is important, in the next step, to gain an understanding of the relationships between the different functions. The starting point of the analysis is the size of the various organizational units; to ensure a well-functioning office environment, the functional and communication relationships must then be established. > Fig. 41 Details to be established include:

— Which organizational units work closely together
— Whether this takes place digitally or requires physical meetings
— How management is to be included in, or separated from, the offices
— Which organizational units should not be far away from other units
— Which organizational units have a strong need for communication and meeting areas
— Which organizational units can also share such areas
— Which areas can be entered directly by visitors and whether semi-public buffer zones, such as meeting points or meeting zones, should be provided
— Which areas may only be entered by visitors and external colleagues with an appropriate authorization

These functional relationships should be very carefully established in conversations with the users, because the current situation often does not represent what is really required or makes sense. Therefore the actual need must be established at the outset.

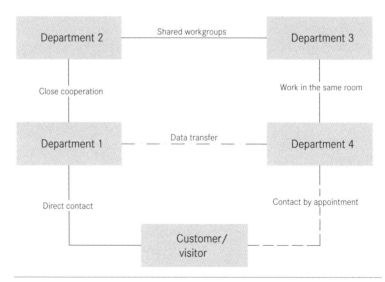

Fig. 41: Diagram identifying relationships between departments

Functional drawings and diagrams are helpful means of visualizing functional relationships. They show the organizational units and ancillary areas in diagrammatic form, and link these with symbols for physical relationships and internal processes. > Fig. 42 In addition, the need for spaces and zoning — for example, "internal/with visitor traffic," "first floor/to be arranged throughout," or "quiet work/communication areas" — can be indicated (e.g. by using color highlighting). A well-executed functional diagram is not only a good communication tool for discussions with the building owner/users, but it also serves as a basis for the subsequent design process, possibly even a helpful intermediate step for designing the building layout. ■

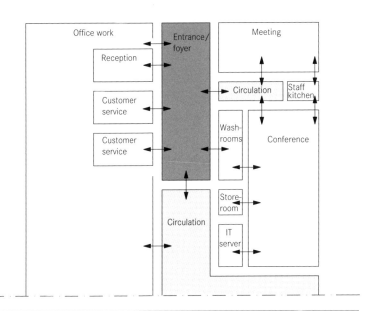

Fig. 42: Section of a functional diagram of an entrance area

■ **Tip:** Functional drawings can be produced in such a way that only the relationships are shown. In a further step, the areas with their actual space requirement can be added, which provides an idea of the proportional spaces, even though it may make it more difficult to clearly see the relationships. In the case of multi-story projects, it may be useful to produce an isometric drawing showing the stories above each other.

In addition to the interaction between organizational units and/or the public, a functional diagram should also show the relationships with ancillary and circulation areas. To this end, the areas discussed in the chapter on ancillary rooms have to be appropriately integrated in the functional diagram for the building. Ancillary rooms such as sanitary facilities, copier rooms and staff kitchens should be located conveniently close to the workplaces, i.e. decentralized. Meeting and conference zones can also be decentralized, e.g. those for short internal meetings, or located centrally, where larger meetings and/or customer contact are involved.

URBAN DESIGN CONTEXT

Once the functional relationships have been established, it is possible to start the development of plan layouts and the design of the building; at this stage it is important to take into account the urban design context, as this is another important design parameter.

In an urban context, the permitted volume of a building or the maximum footprint area are often given parameters. This may be in the form of a land-use plan that specifies the type of development permitted on the plot, or may be determined by the local context, as when a gap in a block-edge development with a given height is to be filled in, for example.

A number of parameters that determine the use of the building plot have to be taken into account. These are the most common:

— The orientation of the plot towards the street/other access points
— The orientation of the plot towards the sun
— The orientation of the plot towards sources of noise, such as a busy road
— Minimum distances required to neighboring buildings
— Special visual connections from and to the public surroundings
— Accessibility via private and public local transport
— The layout of parking areas

Plots sometimes come in very specific geometric layouts, which thereby affect the type of building. Sometimes the immediately neighboring buildings (such as in a block-edge development) are the deciding factor for the position and orientation of the building. Even where there are few limiting factors owing to the shape of the plot or the context, there may still be other factors that have to be considered. These may include the orientation towards a public space or park area, the visual effect of the building in the street context, protection against noise in the case of very busy roads, the orientation of the building to maximize daylight, and many others.

Access to the building plot is often a critical parameter, particularly in the urban context. For pedestrian access, proximity to the public local transport network is important; for vehicular access, a considerable amount of space needs to be dedicated to driveways and parking areas. Where it is not possible to provide parking areas at ground level on the plot, it may be necessary to provide underground parking garages next to or underneath the building. > Chapter Design concept and building types, Room types and structural systems

Access to the building plot

○

BUILDING TYPES

Traditionally, the design of office buildings is mostly determined by a rational building depth and the possibilities for providing lighting. This has led to the development of different building shapes, which can be found again and again in different guises.

The most common building shapes are the ribbon building or the slab building, which allow daylight to enter at the long sides, and are therefore very well suited for linear office arrangements. Both ribbon buildings and slab buildings usually feature a central corridor (double-loaded) or two corridors with a combi-zone between them (triple-loaded). > Fig. 43 and Chapter Design concept and building types, Circulation systems Owing to their poor efficiency in terms of use of floor area, single-loaded buildings are only used where lighting from both sides is not possible, natural lighting of

Ribbon or slab buildings

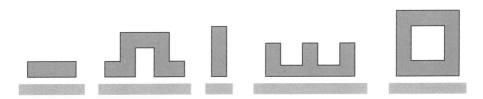

Fig. 43: Examples of positioning an office building towards the public street space

○ **Note**: The minimum number of parking spaces required for buildings with general offices and administration rooms may be specified in the locally applicable building code and should be discussed with the stakeholders involved. For example, the building code for North Rhine-Westphalia specifies a minimum of one parking space for every 30 to 40 m^2 of usable office floor area. This includes a proportion of visitor spaces of 20%. Staff rooms and sanitary facilities, as well as functional and circulation areas, are not included in the usable office floor area.

the corridor is wanted, or the corridor zone is needed as a buffer against noise emissions. It is also possible to combine ribbon buildings with each other, or with other shapes of buildings. Usually this is achieved using appropriately designed central circulation cores. Depending on the depth of the building, ribbon buildings or slab buildings are suitable for cellular, group, or combi-offices.

Point-block buildings Point-block buildings usually only have one central circulation core, and are considered very efficient in terms of use of space because the corridor area is kept to a minimum. However, as the building increases in height, this space efficiency reduces because the circulation areas have to be larger for higher buildings and this size has to be adopted on all floors. > Fig. 44 Point-block buildings are suitable for cellular, group, open-plan, and combi-offices.

☐ Vertical circulation
▨ Functional area
■ Horizontal circulation

Fig. 44: Examples of ribbon buildings (double- and triple-loaded)

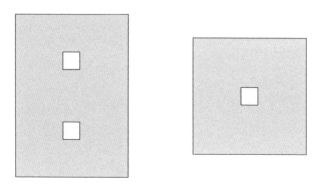

Fig. 45: Examples of point-block buildings

Block-edge and courtyard buildings usually enclose protected, quiet Block-edge buildings/ courtyard buildings inner courtyards and consist of ribbon-type tracts enclosing this court-yard. > Fig. 46 Although courtyard buildings provide the opportunity for high-quality interiors, the lighting situation on the lower floors can be quite restricted in the case of smaller courtyards. These internal court-yards can also be used as communication areas or even canteens, thus considerably improving the quality of the entire building, but on the down-side there are additional noise emissions to be taken into account. Block-edge and courtyard buildings are suitable for cellular, group, open-plan, and combi-offices; it may also be possible to link them with point-block tower buildings.

Spine-and-fingers buildings are similar in structure to courtyard Spine-and-fingers buildings buildings, except that their courtyards are open to the surroundings on one side. > Fig. 47 It is relatively easy to extend an existing ribbon building to create a spine-and-fingers building; this will retain the closed building front towards the street but benefit from open facades at the rear to-wards the landscape. There are various methods of combining these forms, which result in a wide range of designs. These buildings too are suitable for cellular, group, open-plan, and combi-offices.

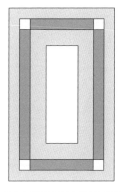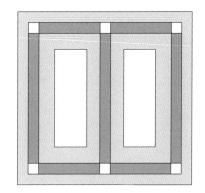

Fig. 46: Examples of block-edge buildings

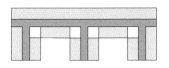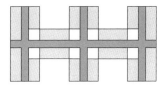

Fig. 47: Examples of spine-and-fingers buildings

In addition to the types of buildings described above, with their rather orthogonal or linear organization, it is also possible to design a wide range of free-form buildings, which may be particularly suited to new office environments. > Fig. 48 Such free-form shapes may be a response to a specific urban context, or can be constructed as freestanding buildings in their own right. They can be developed as completely free or amorphous structures, or may just feature those free-form shapes in their footprint layout. Functional layouts with open-plan designs or combi-zones can be used to create different building depths while also offering the opportunity to design interesting circulation and communication areas. Free-form shapes present a challenge for the interior fit-out and furnishing, because it may be necessary, depending on the concept, to produce purpose-built elements.

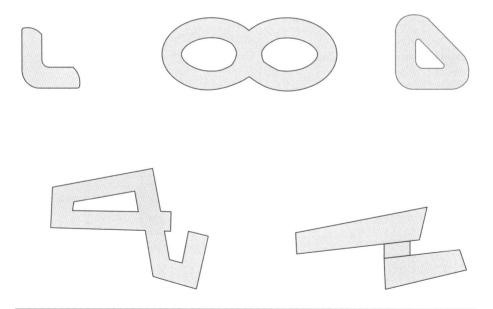

Fig. 48: Examples of free-form buildings

CIRCULATION SYSTEMS

Efficient and clearly structured circulation is essential for providing access to all areas. Each functional unit should be accessible directly via the entrance area, and through internal circulation areas such as staircases, elevators, corridors, and, if necessary, lobbies, in order to avoid passing through other departments and the causing a disturbance. > Chapter Room typologies, Circulation and services In many cases, all important access and ancillary functions are located in central circulation cores. These can be arranged in vertical alignment to allow for the most efficient circulation routes and services installations.

Access to organizational units

A distinction in layout typology is made between single-loaded, double-loaded, triple-loaded, and corridor-less circulation systems. > Fig. 49

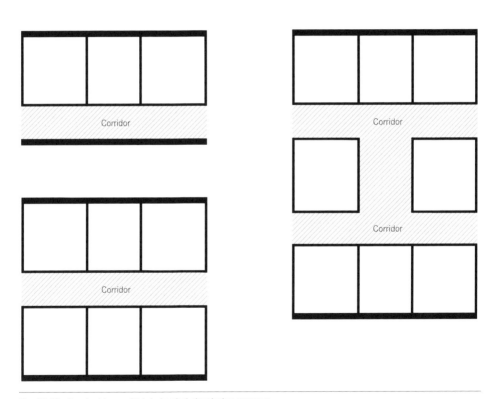

Fig. 49: Single-, double-, and triple-loaded circulation systems

In a single-loaded circulation situation, the corridor is located to one side of the building along the facade, with offices arranged along the other side. > Fig. 50 This means that the corridors benefit from full daylight. This type of layout is suitable for buildings with a high number of visitors, for arrangements facing an atrium or in an industrial situation, for narrow building plots that only have room for a shallow building depth, or for creating a buffer zone in order to protect the workplaces from noise emissions from very busy roads. However, buildings with single-loaded corridors have an unfavorable proportion of usable floor area to circulation area, and are therefore usually inefficient in terms of use of space.

As a rule, the circulation in traditional office buildings consists of double-loaded corridors. This means that a central corridor provides access to cellular or group offices on both sides. > Fig. 51 Although this type of organization is very efficient in terms of use of space, it does mean that ancillary functions have to be located along the "expensive" facade areas. Furthermore, the corridor is internal and therefore cannot receive any natural light unless there are zones without offices or the separating walls to the offices are transparent.

In triple-loaded circulation systems, two internal corridors provide access to offices along the outside of the building. > Fig. 52 The middle or combi-zone between the corridors is used to accommodate the vertical circulation, as well as ancillary rooms such as staff kitchens, communication zones, archive and media rooms, and sanitary facilities. > Fig. 53

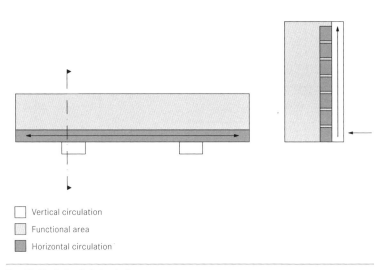

☐ Vertical circulation
▨ Functional area
■ Horizontal circulation

Fig. 50: Single-loaded circulation

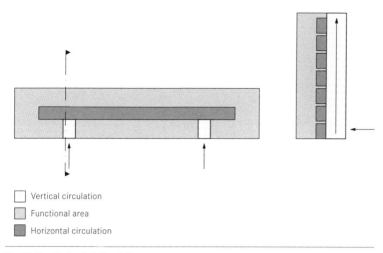

☐ Vertical circulation

▨ Functional area

■ Horizontal circulation

Fig. 51: Double-loaded circulation

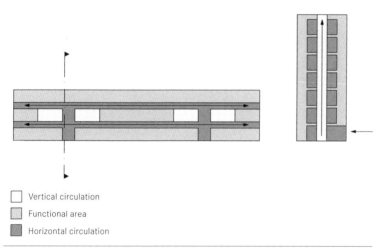

☐ Vertical circulation

▨ Functional area

■ Horizontal circulation

Fig. 52: Triple-loaded circulation

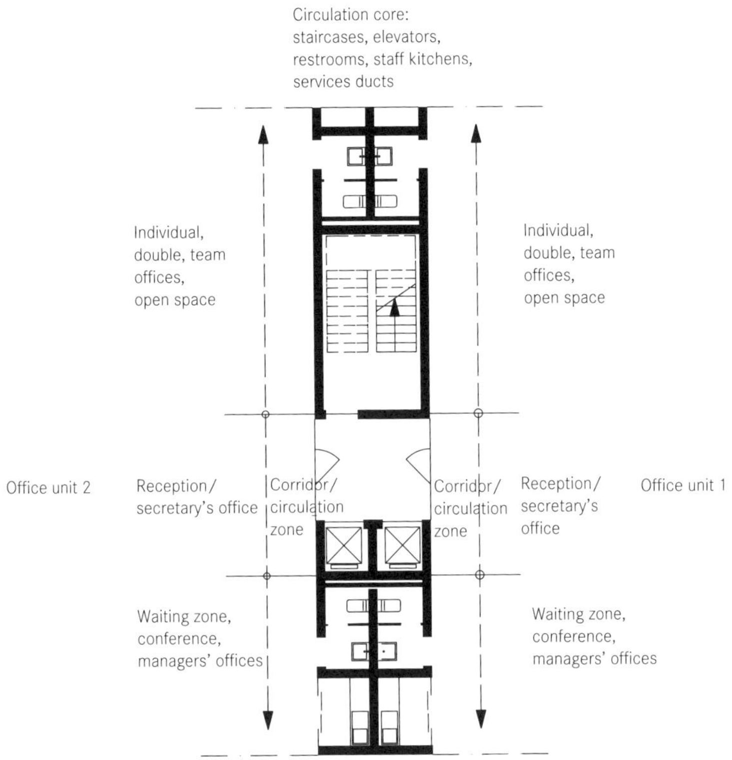

Circulation core:
staircases, elevators,
restrooms, staff kitchens,
services ducts

Individual,
double, team
offices,
open space

Individual,
double, team
offices,
open space

Office unit 2

Reception/
secretary's office

Corridor/
circulation
zone

Corridor/
circulation
zone

Reception/
secretary's
office

Office unit 1

Waiting zone,
conference,
managers' offices

Waiting zone,
conference,
managers' offices

Fig. 53: Typical elements of the interior zone in a triple-loaded layout

In this way it is possible to create compact buildings with a smaller external facade envelope. On the other hand, ventilation and lighting of the interior areas is not possible via natural means, which means that mechanical installations have to be provided.

Circulation system without corridors   Circulation systems without corridors are traditionally used in open-plan office and point-block buildings. > Fig. 54 These are considered to be very efficient in terms of use of space, as the space requirement for circulation is much reduced; however, emergency evacuation and rescue routes must also be provided in open-plan offices and be kept clear of furniture. As a rule, high-rise office blocks with corridor-less circulation systems do not make very efficient use of the available space because the vertical circulation for all employees and customers needs to be arranged with redundant elements, such as elevators, as do the installations for media and services.

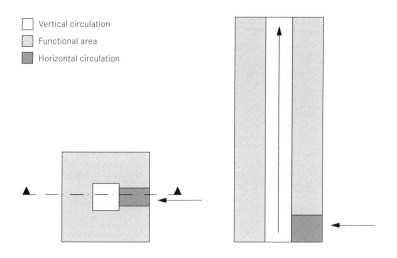

Fig. 54: Circulation system without corridors

Vertical circulation

Functional area

Horizontal circulation

ROOM TYPES AND STRUCTURAL SYSTEMS

In most cases, the structural systems of office buildings consist of skeleton constructions with grids of columns. In view of the fact that the structure of an office building needs to suit the depth and subdivision of the building, it is appropriate to consider the structural system at an early stage. In many cases the structural system determines the segmentation of the facade and the possible fit-out grid on the interior of the building.

If one develops the depth of the building on the basis of providing adequate natural light to the offices, the depth of cellular offices should not be more than 5.00 to 7.00 m because otherwise the back of the rooms would be very dark. If larger types of offices are used, it is possible to provide a room depth of up to 10 m or more. > Tab. 12 Taking the dimension on the room depth, it is possible to calculate the depth of the building by adding the width of corridors and any combi-zones, as well as the depth required for construction elements. > Fig. 55

Room and building depths

○

○ **Note**: The depth to which natural lighting is effective for workplaces can be calculated by multiplying the height of the window by a factor of approx. 1.5. If cabinets and/or additional internal connecting doors are provided in the rear part of the offices, it is possible for the room and building depth of buildings with cellular and group offices to be greater, because these intercommunication areas can be located towards the interior of the building where natural lighting is reduced.

Tab. 12: Room and building depths for different types of offices

Type of office	Room depth of office	Building depth depending on the type of circulation		
		Single-loaded	Double-loaded	Triple-loaded
Cellular office	5 to 7 m	7–11 m	12–18 m	19–26 m
Group office	5 to 10 m	7–14 m	12–24 m	22–32 m
Combi-office (cellular and group offices)	5 to 10 m			22–28 m
Open-plan and non-territorial office environments	15 to 30 m	Same as the building depth, excluding depth of construction elements		

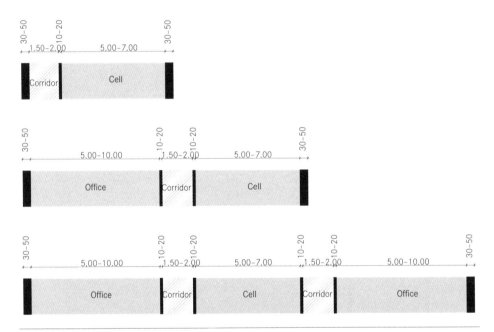

Fig. 55: Determining the building depth for different circulation systems

Structural and bracing systems   If the building has been designed using skeleton construction, the columns are usually arranged in the interior and along the facades. The interior rows of columns can be arranged centrally or spread out to suit the respective floor layout, e.g. to avoid placing columns where there is a central corridor. In designs with flat floor slabs without downstand beams, the exterior rows of columns are usually moved away from the facade by between 40 and 80 cm towards the interior to better transfer the loads of the floor slabs to the columns. Loadbearing walls are generally only used in cores with a bracing function, but can sometimes also be used in the external building envelope. ∎

A basic distinction is made between a structural grid, a facade grid, Types of grids and a fit-out grid. The structural grid is defined by the positions of the columns and the distance between them. The facade and fit-out grids are usually determined by subdividing the structural grid to accommodate the smaller divisions required in facades and in fit-out elements. The structural grid should be a multiple of the facade and fit-out grids, so as to avoid construction problems and overlaps. In many designs, the dimension of the structural grid is five to eight times the dimension of the basic fit-out grid.

Facade and fit-out grids are usually identical, but one may also be twice the size of the other. As a rule, the grid axes are vertically aligned. However, depending on the design concept, the structural grid can be offset by half a grid dimension. > Fig. 56 The advantage of this is that the columns do not have to be integrated into the external walls; the disadvantage is that they are located in the room, and thus reduce the flexibility of the use of space.

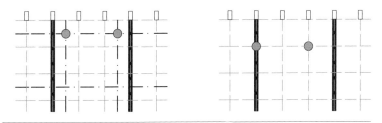

Fig. 56: Examples of structural, fit-out, and facade grids superimposed

∎ **Tip:** In the volume *Basics Loadbearing Systems* by Alfred Meistermann, the basic relationships between conceptual design ideas and structural systems are discussed, as well as the basic relationships between the application of forces, load assumptions, and structural systems.

Tab. 13: Typical grid dimensions in office and administration buildings

0.5 × grid	1 × grid	1.5 × grid	2 × grid	3 × grid	4 × grid	5 × grid	6 × grid	7 × grid	....
0.60 m	1.20 m	1.80 m	2.40 m	3.60 m	4.80 m	6.00 m	7.20 m	8.40 m	....
0.625 m	1.25 m	1.875 m	2.50 m	3.75 m	5.00 m	6.25 m	7.50 m	8.75 m	....
0.675 m	1.35 m	2.025 m	2.70 m	4.05 m	5.40 m	6.75 m	8.10 m	9.45 m	....
0.75 m	1.50 m	2.25 m	3.00 m	4.50 m	6.00 m	7.50 m	9.00 m	10.50 m	....

Grid dimensions

Typically, grids are based on multiples of the basic dimensions of 1.20 m, 1.35 m, or 1.50 m. > Tab. 13 When choosing a basic grid dimension, the intended design of the offices and workplaces should be taken into account in order to use the available space as efficiently as possible, for example to achieve the optimum room width of cellular offices.
> Chapter Room typologies, Office types

With larger basic grid dimensions, the office rooms also become more comfortable, with higher quality interiors; however, the space efficiency is reduced. > Figs. 57–59

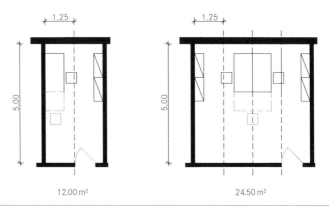

12.00 m²   24.50 m²

Fig. 57: Space requirements of single and double offices based on a fit-out grid of 1.25 m

■ **Tip**: As a rule, fit-out grids of 1.20 m are not very useful because, owing to the thickness of partition walls, which must meet acoustic, fire-protection, and noise-reduction requirements, the resulting office rooms are rather narrow, providing poor furnishing options.

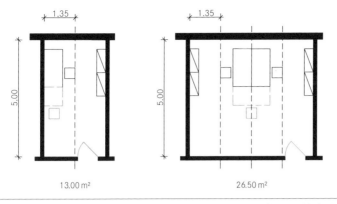

Fig. 58: Space requirements of single and double offices based on a fit-out grid of 1.35 m

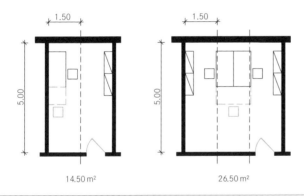

Fig. 59: Space requirements of single and double offices based on a fit-out grid of 1.50 m

If an underground parking garage is built beneath the office build- Structural system
ing, the columns and walls of the office building should preferably be ver- of underground
tically aligned with the structural elements of the underground parking parking garages
garage so that loads can be transferred directly to the substrate. However, since the dimensions of underground parking garages follow standard regulations, these dimensions in turn affect the structural system of
the building above. > Fig. 60 A basic building grid dimension of 1.35 m is
often used for buildings above an underground parking garage, because

the dimension of 5.40 m, which is four times the grid dimension, less the column thickness, results in a space that is sufficient for 2 parking spaces of 2.50 m width.

Where a prestigious large foyer or large seminar and conference areas are part of the design, it is necessary to interrupt the structural grid of the floors above, at least partially, and to support the resulting loads. This usually requires larger downstand beams, which must be taken into account in the design of the slab thickness above these areas. Alternatively, it is possible to opt for larger spans throughout the building, even though this results in more costly floor constructions which may not be economically viable. The resulting column-free areas of the offices do, however, provide maximum flexibility in use, particularly for non-territorial office environments and open-plan offices.

Figures 61–63 show some examples of the integration of structural grids in cellular, group and combi-offices.

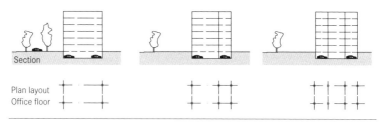

Fig. 60: Alignment of columns in underground parking garages and office floors

■ **Tip:** More detailed information on the design of parking lots and underground parking garages can be found in *Planning Architecture* by Bert Bielefeld, published by Birkhäuser.

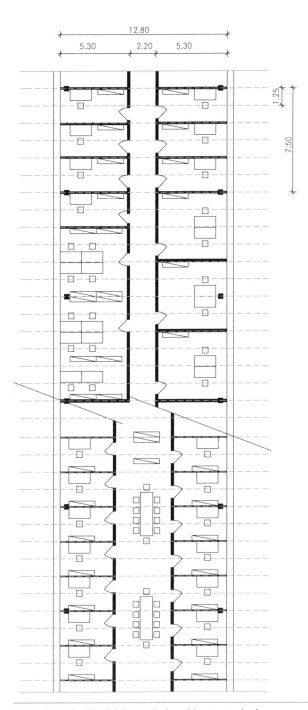

Fig. 61: Example of flexible layout design without central columns

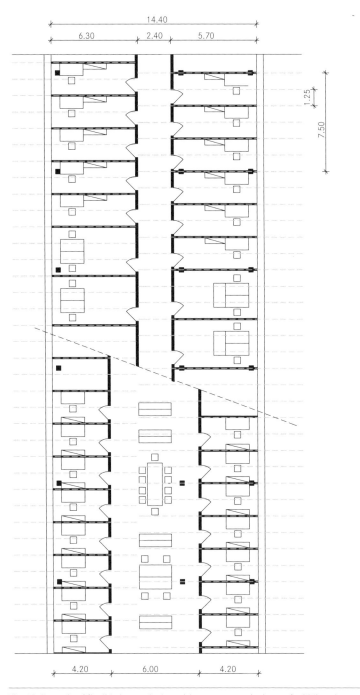

Fig. 62: Example of flexible layout design with an asymmetrical row of middle columns

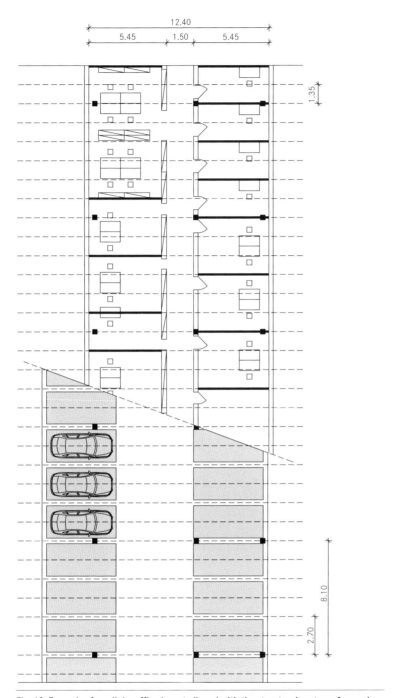

Fig. 63: Example of a cellular office layout aligned with the structural system of an under-ground parking garage

In conclusion

More than other building typologies, the design of office buildings is subject to systematic dependencies and approaches. Depending on the organizational workplaces and the multiplication of workplace layouts, designs are often based on systematic building volumes and structural systems. This may, however, lead to a design approach that is otherwise used for industrial buildings, which would not do justice to today's standards and expectations regarding quality of workspaces and working environments. Furthermore, excessive reliance on systematic designs may lead to an office building design that is unsatisfactory in terms of conceptual appearance and lacks architectural quality.

The information provided here is only intended to provide a basic understanding of the specific framework conditions applicable to office buildings. Equipped with this "tool," the task is to promote the creativity and design quality of one's own project; this also involves questioning traditional standards in office buildings, and may lead to the creation of radical new solutions. In view of the rapid changes currently taking place in the services industry, it is necessary to redefine work environments and office buildings and to flexibly prepare for future challenges.

Appendix

LITERATURE

Bert Bielefeld: *Planning Architecture: Dimensions and Typologies*,
Birkhäuser, Basel 2015

Bert Bielefeld, Sebastian El khouli: *Basics Design Ideas,* Birkhäuser,
Basel 2007

DETAIL: best of DETAIL Büro, 2013

Peter Ebner, Eva Herrmann: *Typology+*, Birkhäuser, Basel 2010

Sharon K. Harmon, Katherine E. Kennon: *The Codes Guidebook for
Interiors*, Wiley, Hoboken 2014

Oliver Klein, Jörg Schlenger: *Basics Room Conditioning*, Birkhäuser,
Basel 2008

Alfred Meistermann: *Basics Loadbearing Systems,* Birkhäuser,
Basel 2007

Ernst Neufert, Peter Neufert: *Architect's Data*, 4th ed., updated
by Johannes Kister et al., translated by David Sturge,
Wiley-Blackwell, Chichester 2012

Ansgar Oswald: *Offices. Construction and Design Manual*, DOM,
Berlin 2013

Isabella Skiba, Rahel Züger: *Basics Barrier-free Planning,* Birkhäuser,
Basel 2009

Roman Skowranek: *Basics Lighting Design*, Birkhäuser, Basel 2017

REGULATIONS AND STANDARDS

German regulations and standards		
ASR A1.2	Technical rules for workplaces Room dimensions and movement areas	2013-09
ASR A1.8	Technical rules for workplaces – Circulation areas	2012-11
ASR A2.3	Technical rules for workplaces – Escape routes and emergency exits, escape and rescue plans	2007-08
ASR A4.2	Technical rules for workplaces – Staff rooms and duty rooms	2012-08
ASR V3a.2	Technical rules for workplaces – Barrier-free design of workplaces	2012-08
DIN 4543-1	Office workplaces – Part 1: Space for the arrangement and use of office furniture; safety requirements	1994-09
DIN 5035-8	Artificial lighting – Part 8: Workplace luminaires – Requirements, recommendations, and tests	2007-07
DIN 15309	Elevators: passenger elevators for buildings other than residential buildings, and bed elevators – Building dimensions, cabin size, door dimensions	2002-06
DIN 16555	Office workplace – Spaces for communication: workplaces in office and administration buildings – Requirements, testing	2002-12
DIN 18040-1	Barrier-free building – Design basics – Part 1: Buildings with public access	2010-10
VDI 2569	Noise protection and acoustic design in offices	2016-02 Draft
VDI 3804	Space ventilation – Office buildings	2009-03
VDI 6000 page 2	Provision of sanitary facilities and their equipment – Workplaces and desks	2007-11 2012-07
DGUV Information 215-443	Acoustics in offices – Aid for the acoustic design of offices	2012-09
BüroFIRL BR	Guideline to space standards in offices	2010-02-23
Licht.wissen 04	Lighting in offices, motivating and efficient	2012-04

Series editor: Bert Bielefeld
Concept: Bert Bielefeld, Annette Gref
Translation from German into English:
Hartwin Busch
English copy editing: Susan James
Project management: Lisa Schulze
Layout, cover design, and typography:
Andreas Hidber
Typesetting: Sven Schrape
Production: Amelie Solbrig

This publication is also available as an e-book (ISBN PDF 978-3-0356-1394-0; ISBN EPUB 978-3-0356-1395-7) and in a German language edition (ISBN 978-3-0356-1380-3).

Library of Congress Cataloging-in-Publication data
A CIP catalog record for this book has been applied for at the Library of Congress.

Bibliographic information published by the German National Library
The German National Library lists this publication in the Deutsche Nationalbibliografie; detailed bibliographic data are available on the Internet at http://dnb.dnb.de.

© 2018 Birkhäuser Verlag GmbH, Basel
P.O. Box 44, 4009 Basel, Switzerland
Part of Walter de Gruyter GmbH, Berlin/Boston

Printed on acid-free paper produced from chlorine-free pulp. TCF ∞

Printed in Germany

ISBN 978-3-0356-1382-7

9 8 7 6 5 4 3 2 1
www.birkhauser.com